Paws For Pauly

This is a true story about a boy, his dog
and the bond of love they share

Written by: Susie Bishop
Illustrated by: Vicki Zanetis

Dedicated to Pauly, Cody and Skippy

Susie Bishop has been an educator for over thirty years. She has shared her unique brand of teaching with countless children by providing patience, love, encouragement, and many, many hugs.

Susie is a children's author, family group conference facilitator, eductional consultant, child advocate and teacher.

She lives in Olney, Illinois and has three children and six grandchildren who provide constant inspiration.

Susie's greatest hope is that parents will take the time to read books daily to their children. Her children's books include - **Who Needs A Bully**, **Eenie Marches From A to Z**, **Eenie Meanie Me and The Very Sad Day** and **Eenie Meanie Me and The Very Scary Day**. Susie's compassion for children and passion for writing are evident in all of her children's books.

Several years ago, Vicki Zanetis started drawing colored pencil portraits of pets for friends and family. As more people saw her work, she had requests to do commercial pet portraits so she started paws2 remember. Her work can be seen at www.paws2remember.biz.

She also taught art at St. Joseph School, grades K-8 for 3 years where she created a program based on the master artists.

Vicki is currently living in Noble, IL with her husband and pets. When she is not pursuing her passion of competition with her cutting horse, she continues to do portraits and illustrations.

Paws For Pauly

A little boy, Pauly, is turning ten

A birthday party, a birthday cake and lots of friends

A birthday present from Roger, the school custodian,

Makes this tenth birthday the very best one

A black and white Beagle pup just six weeks old

Is the very best gift any boy could ever hold

The boy calls the puppy, "Cody," after his best pal

"Cody" is a perfect name for a Beagle who can howl

The boy and his dog become very close

One follows the other tripping over paws and toes

A lick all over the face or a pat on the head

Holding on to each other as they slip into bed

Pauly gives Cody a doggie treat...

Three hot dogs every day just can't be beat

One day when Pauly is away at school

Cody breaks his outside chain and runs off like a fool

He finds Pauly's school and sits

By the door until school is over

Then takes off and beats Pauly home

With a shortcut through the clover

Pauly and Cody became very best buddies

They fish, they play, they hunt and come home all muddy

At night, Pauly tries to slip Cody into his room

But Mommy always knows it's best

Cody is out under the moon

Cody takes a walk while Pauly's at school

He finds a female friend who is very cool

The girlfriend lives just down two streets

Pauly doesn't seem to mind when he takes a backseat

Very soon the girlfriend becomes a mother

And Cody has two puppies who are now Beagle brothers

One is named Hershey; the other one Max

Chewing on anything that comes in their path

Cody licks Pauly's face and the two little pups

They hide Pauly's toys and drool on his stuff

Cody fetches the football as Pauly practices kicking

He runs after tennis balls as his paws go clicking

The time comes for Pauly to learn to drive

The old long bed truck will do just fine

Pauly and Cody practice driving every day

Cody's head is hanging out the window as they go their

Merry way

The boy and his dog growing up together

Life just couldn't get any better.

These two stick together through thick and thin

But one day little boys become teenage men

Cody waits and waits for Pauly to come home

The days are getting longer for a dog all alone

Pauly drives down the lane hoping not to crash

Cody's up and at the gate ... together at last

Cody tries to run, but his legs are getting older

He licks and licks the face of his favorite owner

Now is the time for a boy to leave the nest

Ten big hugs for Cody, whom he loves the best

Pauly's heading off to college at the U of I

My! Oh My! How the time does fly

Cody knows his best pal has gone away

And he dies of a broken heart that very same day

Pauly's daddy buries Cody in a backyard grave

With a small heart cross and Cody's name

VLZ
2014

When Pauly finds out he's lost his very best friend

His heart is very sad, but time will help it mend

Pauly's tears flow when he drives down the lane

No lip-lapping dog to howl and play

He checks out the grave and sees the cross

He kneels and puts a hot dog on the moss

Inseparable friends from the age of ten,

These two bosom buddies will meet again

Pauly finds peace without his doggie brother

This bond of love is like no other

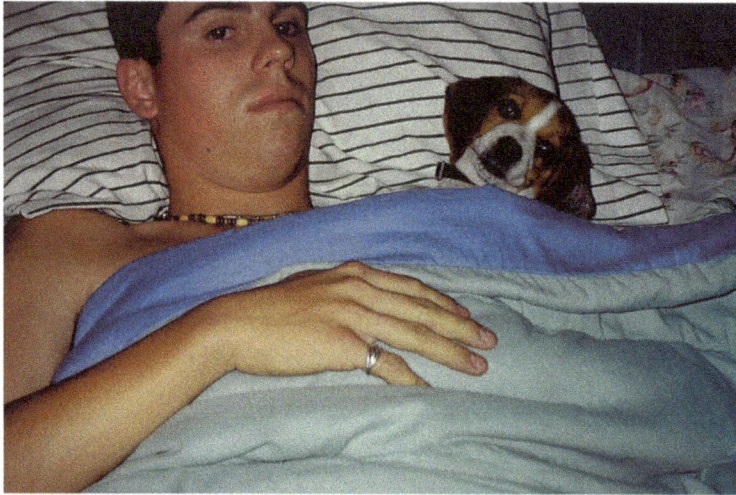

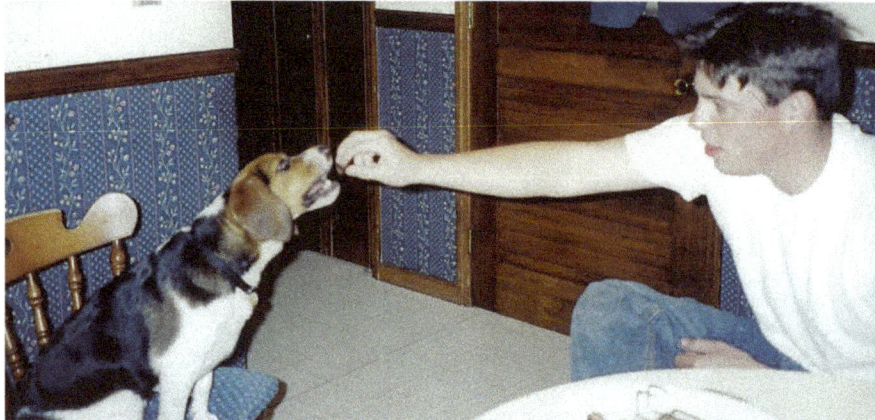

This is a true story about a boy, his dog and the bond of love they share.

PRINT FORCE

PRINTFORCE INC.

1409 EAST MAIN OLNEY, IL 62450

www.printforceinc.com

orders.printforce@gmail.com

PH/FX 618.395.7746

Printed in the United States of America

Olney, IL

This book is printed on acid-free paper

$25.00

ISBN 978-0-9772878-4-0

52500>

9 780977 287840